More Fire

and Other Poems

by John Enright

An Enright House book

Published by Lulu.com

Other books by John Enright:

Starbound And Other Poems

Unholy Quest (novel)

ISBN: 978-1-4303-1403-5

Table of Contents:

Open Your Eyes

Open your eyes
And rise.

Breathe the air
And dare.

Do something great -
Don't wait.

Ayn Rand's Arrival (in America)

Not knowing all the words for what she feels,
She doesn't worry, words and knowledge will come.
In time she thinks, in time, for now she reels,
Giddy with breaths of free air,
          gazing up at the blue dome
Of sky and the towers that scrape it. "What
Evil could lurk here?" she asks. "I can't imagine any.
And even if there were, my bonds are cut
And – Ah! Joy gives me strength!
          Who could defeat me?"

Does anyone stop to stare at the immigrant girl
Who twirls on the sidewalk with those eyes –
So large and brilliant as they sparkle with delight?
Does anyone wonder what strange new surprise
She holds, or guess that someday she will write
A tale to shake the shoulders of the world?

A Writer Named Rand

There once was a writer named Rand
Who never feared taking a stand.
  She staked out positions
  And stocked up munitions!
The fireworks always were grand.

A Philosopher Named David Kelley

A philosopher named David Kelley,
Appeared on a show on the telly.
  He said greed is good
  And that we all should
Say to heck with that nun from New Delhi.

Benevolence

Benevolence
Looks over the fence.

Pride
Looks inside.

The Benevolent Universe

Among Objectivists the belief is prevalent
That the Universe is somehow benevolent.
Not just this planet, but the whole damn thing.
Well, I don't mind including Saturn's rings,
But I'm not too sure about those big black holes.
I mean, suppose I'm happily pursuing goals
But I fall into a point singularity,
Which has this physical peculiarity:
That no matter how much I scream and shout,
No one can ever pull me out!
A horrid hole that makes you sink so -
Does that sound benevolent to you?
   I didn't think so.

Painting In Depth (for Michael Newberry)

To draw the world's lines,
To paint the places where it's dark
And where it shines.

Whether lush or stark
To let it leap
Into space.

So deep - it seems a dream,
More real than real.

At last you see and feel
The secret face of life.

With a Flourish

Objectivists agree
That in the case of "to be or not to be"
It's better to be.

But some of them argue whether the key
Is simply surviving
Or amply thriving.

From the outside looking in,
I bet it gives the impression
Of that great Medieval question:
How many angels can fit on the head of a pin?

I mean, either way, thrive or survive,
You have to be alive.

Explaining Postmodernism
(For Stephen Hicks)

The socialist left
was bereft
of success.
But they didn't say "Yes,
We were wrong."

Instead they sang this song:

"Of perception, let's be leery,
Since it's all based on a theory,
And the law of contradiction
Is a frightful sort of fiction,
So we're opting for defiance
Of the principles of science.
Which enables us to say:
Socialism's here to stay!"

Why Did Dagny Fall For Galt?

Why did Dagny fall for Galt?
(Falling right out of the skies.)
Was her judgment simply at fault
For ditching those other guys?

It must have been something about his face
That made her heart go tilt -
Eyes that didn't bear a trace
Of pain or fear or guilt.

What was it about his identity
That swept her off her feet?
I put the blame on serenity -
That made her feel complete.

Now, you may think that Galt's unreal,
And I don't wish to argue the question,
But whatever he was, he made Dagny feel
Something approaching obsession.

Galt

Unknown hero, walking through the pages
Of your own book - the man of mystery -
Quietly talking while the battle rages,
Working in silence to alter history.
They ask if you are human or a god -
Impervious to passion - so it seems.
A face without a trace of pain? How odd.
How can it be no nightmares haunt your dreams?
You see too far. The world's complex course
Spins out for you as algebraic proof,
From first equation through to final force.
Ahead of time, alone, you stand aloof.
As lightning stands against the blinded sky.
Not motionless. Just faster than the eye.

Second Coming, for Susan McCloskey

Last night I had the strangest dream.
I greatly fear the food
I ate at dinner was at fault
For my uneasy mood.
I stood in heaven – so it seemed.
I stood beside Lord Jesus.
He said "To be compared to Galt
Really doesn't please us."

He said that He'd read Atlas Shrugged
When he was back in college
But hadn't cared too much for Galt
And his all-perfect knowledge.
He said that He was badly bugged
When Dagny's tale was done.
He'd hoped that at her story's halt
She would become a nun.

She'd be the perfect Bride of Christ
Bewitching and bedeviling.
"Beatitudes be damned!" He said,
"I'm tired of all this leveling.
I'm sick of all this sacrifice.
It's really got to go!
Why wait to live until you're dead?
No reason that I know!"

Just then a giant cloud of smoke
Swallowed the Redeemer,
And slowly it occurred to me
That I was just a dreamer,
That all the startling words he spoke
Were caused by the suggestion
Of lectures heard quite recently
Combined with indigestion.

Lecture Notes

Someday I'll give a lecture
On Rand and architecture.
I'll postulate with unction,
That form should follow function,
But that getting rid of ornament
Wasn't really what she meant.

What's hard to convey
Is the "takes your breath away".
If that means nothing to you,
There's not much I can do
With Powerpoint slides
Of a building's insides.

An Open and Shut Case

I dreamed I saw the ghost of Rand
Wandering angry across the land.
I asked her what was wrong, and she
Said "A.R.I. and T.O.C.!
Frankly, I critique them both.
Open? Closed? I roundly loathe
All such false dichotomies.
Search my works and you will see
Just how clearly I declined
To say I had an open mind;
Nor did I say my mind was closed;
I said the choice was badly posed,
And that the true alternative
Was keep an ACTIVE mind, and live!"

Case Reopened

The dream is fled.
That spirited lecture,
What the ghost said,
Was pure conjecture.

And no one knows
If she'd lend her voice
To open or closed
Or some other choice.

Atlantis World, a musical without music

Setting: Opening day at a new amusement park

Song 1, sung by heroine and chorus

Welcome to this wondrous place
We call Atlantis World!
Today's the day our brand new shining
Flag will be unfurled:
A golden dollar sign
Upon a field of brilliant white,
To show this land at last has been
Redeemed from mystic night.

Atlantis, Atlantis,
Enlighten, enchant us!
It's what we all need,
A valley of greed!

Since Atlas Shrugged the movie
Proved to be a huge success
A theme-park tie in had to be
An overwhelming yes.
The nation's children really want
To be just like John Galt:
Without a trace of pain or fear,
Without a trace of fault.

Atlantis, Atlantis,
Enlighten, enchant us!
Where it's safe to say
That A will stay A!

Old fashioned Barbie dolls
Can't turn a profit for Mattel.
New Dagny Taggart dolls
Are now the only ones that sell.
She comes with her own railroad set,
Along with a trench coat,
And three exciting hero dolls,
Who each can float her boat.

Atlantis, Atlantis,
Enlighten, enchant us!
The only real treason
Is forsaking reason!

So, join us, in this joyous place
We call Atlantis World!
Get on our airplane ride
And you will suddenly be hurled
Into a big crash landing,
But we'll make sure you survive.
For after all, our ethic says
It's good to be alive!

Atlantis, Atlantis,
Enlighten, enchant us!
A kingdom of cash
Where goals never clash!

Song 2, sung by the villain of the piece

I'm here to stop the motor
Of this unamusing park.

I'm here to turn its lights off
And to plunge it into dark.
Objectivism must be taken
Very seriously.
It's wrong to celebrate it
So goddamned deliriously.

I'll dynamite
This place tonight.
I'll blow it sky high.
Atlantis, goodbye.

It's an abomination
Of the author's own intent,
A horribly distorted twist
On what the novel meant,
And just as Howard Roark was right
To blow up public housing,
I'm right to give this creepy park
A general delousing.

I'll blow apart
This anti-art.
I'll blow it sky high.
Atlantis, goodbye.

The roller coaster ride they built,
They call the John Galt Line.
It runs on rails of green blue metal –
Through a copper mine.
I've rigged it to explode as soon
As I push down this button.
The blast will rip this ride apart –
Reducin' it to nuttin'!

I'll undefine
This John Galt Line.
I'll blow it sky high.
Atlantis, goodbye.

Song 3, duet, sung by villain and heroine.

She:
Oh, won't you try the John Galt Line.
Please give it just one try.
Get first-hand evidence before
You blow it all sky-high.

He:
My mind's made up. I've seen the facts.
My judgment's very strong.
With full contextual certainty,
I'm hardly ever wrong.

She:
But seeing it is not the same
As giving it a try.
Oh, please just ride it once before
You blow it all sky high.

He:
I know I'm right. I know I'm right.
I do not need more facts.
Stand back while I demolish these
Unholy green blue tracks.

She:
So what's the matter, are you scared
Of facing your own guilt?
Afraid of finding out this ride's
The best one ever built?

He:
All right! All right! I'll ride it once.
I'll verify my claims.
I'll give it just one try before
It all goes down in flames.

Song 4, heroine and chorus sing:

It's all aboard the John Galt line!
The ribbon has been sliced!
It only costs one dollar,
So you see it's fairly priced!
There's just one catch, one little catch,
Which must be squarely told:
It only costs a dollar, but –
You have to pay in gold!

We're gliding on the John Galt line,
We're gliding out the station.
We're picking up velocity –
With smooth acceleration.
There's something odd about this train
We mustn't fail to mention:
It gets its power from a strange
Antenna on the engine!

Song 5, villain sings:

The landscape seems to fall away.
I hear the engines roar.
A pulsing power fills my heart.
I feel my spirits soar.
I sense that man should never be
Held down by groundless fear.
Behold! We climb into a sky
So cloudless, free and clear.

What's this? The roller coaster dives!
This wasn't in the book.
The ground is rushing up at us.
I cannot stand to look.
I can't believe the bravery
Of Dagny's dauntless brain.
How did she maintain open eyes
While plunging in a plane?

Whoa-oh! We swoop! We rise back up.
We're not dead after all.
We rise. We are the rising.
Can you hear the music call?
The notes speak of a struggle
That I've somehow left behind.
Harmonious serenity
Is spreading through my mind.

The ride is slowing to a stop.
It's time to end this song.
I hate to say it, but it's true,
I see that I was wrong.
I take back all my threats.

This park is full of life and fun.
Now I just want to stay and play.
I guess this story's done.

Song 6, chorus sings as heroine and redeemed villain kiss
passionately

Atlantis, Atlantis,
Where love is romantic
It starts antagonistic
But it ends up hot and frantic!

Kant

I really want
To understand Kant
And all of his vaunted system.
But somehow my brain resists him.

I'd like to take the helm
On a trip through his noumenal realm
And soak up all the glories
Of his cognitive categories.

But somehow my mind cries: "No!
It's no place you want to go.
It's just a Jurassic Park
Where monstrous things lurk in the dark."

Lookout Point

The city stands astride the river's mouth
Where swampland for uncounted centuries
Lay flat in soggy sleep. Miles to the south
Atop a ridge, above a spread of trees,
I stand, and gaze upon the awesome towers
That seem to float like clouds, but never move.
Day after day they're there, through all the hours
And all the years, solid, as if to prove -
That all is possible - that living dreams
Can be achieved - made real in stone and steel.
The birds fly overhead and, far above,
A jet roars 'cross the sky. The sunlight gleams
Upon its wings, and all that I can feel
Is happy in the power of my love.

More Fire

Serenity is wonderful, and quiet contemplation
Should be a part of everybody's life.
But in own my experience, a jolt of raw sensation
Can be a better help in times of strife.

It's nice to be above it all. It's nice to feel complete.
It's great to sense the oneness in all things.
But when survival hinges on your power to compete,
You'll need the force that only passion brings.

When meditation's over and the time has come to act,
Let hot desires energize your brain.
A candle flame is peaceful, but you'll find that it's a fact:
You need more fire to face the wind and rain.

Zero Visibility

She stood at the top of the hill in her skis
Unable to see all the way to her knees.
A whirling white world - blinded by snow -
Without any out but to push off and go.

So, trusting to balance, and banking on skill,
She thrust herself forward and surged with the thrill
Of gliding along that invisible slope -
Coasting on courage, happy with hope.

Labyrinth

Gladly you walked the maze with me;
Though it was dark, though I could hear
The roaring of the Minotaur,
You stood beside me in my fear.

And when it grew too dark to see
What lay ahead, your voice was clear.
And so I stepped as one who slept,
And waked to find you standing near.

Why Tri

To swim, to bike, to run,
somehow it captures
the spirit of a child's
summer day.

Beneath the radiant sun
to feel the rapture
of racing, free and wild,
all the way.

April First

I've finally decided that since rhyme is much derided (as a tool that's too delirious for expression that is serious) that in fact I really ought to confine my written thought to the form that everyone knows is perfect for that: prose. Or, if I'm feeling terse, I might deign to write a verse, but I'll keep it free of rhyme by avoiding words that chime, in a certain charming form with a strict and ancient norm. Tell me, please, how like you the syllables of haiku?

Daffodils trumpet
March's roaring departure.
No April fools they.

Sunset

Streaks of pink and purple in the sky
Make me think of blue- and raspberry pie.
Although it wasn't on my list of wishes,
It's great to taste a sunset turned delicious.
Soon the sun will sink to something duller,
So seize the instant - gobble up the color!

Vermeer's Girl With A Pearl Earring

A turban-wearing girl
With an earring made of pearl
Looks out with shining eyes
With a glance of sweet surprise
As if she's glad you're there.
And you wonder if her hair
When finally unbound
Could match the beauty found
In the sparkle of her gaze
In the glory of the rays
Of sun that bathe the girl
With an earring made of pearl.

Commuter Train

Just the idea of laying steel track,
Evenly spaced, there and back,
Boggles the brain.

But then - to build a train?
That makes the laying
Of track... seem like mere playing.

Harnessing explosive forces
To out-pull a thousand horses...
How exactly is that done?

I wonder whether I'm the only one
Who's awestruck, as we glide along the rails,
At just how rarely this thunder beast fails.

Math (for Marty Lewinter)

Math can seem a cold, hard path,
Alien and aloof.

But when you grasp a proof,
The numbers and the lines
Transform to something warm
And glowing.

There's nothing more divine
Than really knowing.

Emergent

It's not that the whole
Gains a mystical soul.

It's just that we're surprised
Once the parts get organized.

Free Money

Nigerians keep sending me offers
To share ill-gotten wealth - to fill my coffers
With somebody's else's inheritance.
These Not-So-Good Samaritans
Intrude upon my existence
With repetitive insistence
That cash in large amounts
Will be wired to my accounts -
But first they need from me
A little fee.

Whatever shall I do?
It's almost too good to be true!

Eminent Domain

They blustered and blew
And the Pig's house fell down.
He cried "What can I do?
The Wolves run the town!"

The Wolves said: "Stay cool.
You don't have to holler.
We'll look at that rule.
For now… here's a dollar."

The Supremes Strike Again

Can anyone tell me
        what the deal with the Supreme Court is?
I mean, I'm not even sure what a "tort" is.
But how can it be "public use" at all
For a town to rip down my house to put up a mall?

And how can "interstate commerce" refer to weed
That people grew and smoked themselves?
I'm tempted to say these judges need to read
The dictionaries sitting on their shelves!

No Surprise

Medicare Costs Skyrocket!
When you pick Peter's pockets
To pay for drugs for Paul,
Is the future hard to call?

Paul buys more:
Bills Soar!

Poor Venus

The Venus de Milo – just who took her arms?
Didn't ancient museums have decent alarms -
At least, say, some watch dogs to bark up a storm?
Without any arms, she can't even stay warm:
Her clothes have all dropped –
       draped down by her waist,
Her breasts are exposed - which is not in good taste.
Until she gets dressed, keep her off of TV
Or she'll get busted by the FCC.

Living Will

If it's plain my brain has died,
Please don't stick a tube inside
My guts to keep my body fed.

That's just nuts. I'd rather be dead.

The Missing Bride

The doe-eyed bride -
She disappeared.
The worst, of course, was instantly feared.

The media was on the case
Plastering her fiancé's face
All over the TV.

Just between you and me,
He looked as guilty as could be.

Then the bride - she reappeared!
Not at all dead, as we had feared.

All she had was a case of cold feet.
She had booked out of town by taking a seat
On a bus headed west.

I guess the poor thing was a bit overstressed.

Note on bridal etiquette:
If you must run away, please let
Someone know
Before you go.

Spare your fiancé the grilling
About the dastardly killing.

Museums

Tour guides chant.
Your brain goes numb.
Blabbing is violence.

Give beauty a chance
To strike you dumb.
Worship in silence.

Thundergod

I.

He never was the wisest god, but Thor
Excelled at battling giants.
Hurling his hammer,
Flinging his defiance,
He toppled towering foes.

How do you suppose
He did it?
Strong? Yes. Well armed? Of course.
And though not wise, he had a kind of cunning.

But what was simply stunning was the force
With which he threw himself
Wholehearted into the fray.

Bolting forward in a blazing blur,
Striking evildoers long before
They knew what hit them.

That was Thor.

II.

Thunder.
Lightning.
Crackling and booming in the air.

When you stop being scared,
You wonder
What kind of god is that?

What power has seized the earth and spoken here?

And when your wonder
Turns to science,
When your fear
Turns to reliance on your brain,
You stand out in the rain
And fly a kite,
Daring the power to strike the string,
So you can capture it and prove
That what makes the sky shake
Is the same stuff that makes
Dead frogs move.

III.

They tamed it,
And they named it
Electricity.

It was tricky.

Like harnessing a wild horse
Whose kick could kill
With shocking force.

What tricks they made it do!
Messages, motors, lights!
Cities shining and buzzing through the night!

And then… machines that almost seemed to think,
As circuits ran in silent calculation,
Crunching information
In the blink of an eye.

All this from flashing brilliance in the sky.

IV.

Solid state circuits
Flip bits
Guiding trajectories.

Cruise missiles glide.

Onboard computers
With satellite feed
Run the equations.

Nowhere to hide.

It's ours
This power.
This hammer of Thor.

Striking like lightning.

Let's try to use it wisely
And what's more,
Let evildoers think twice
Before they bring us war.

Gelatinous

The gelatinous thing on the chair
Gently smiled at me.
Its eyes seemed to say "Yes, I care,
Won't you sit on my knee?"

I gingerly placed my behind
Where its knee should have been.
I tried to sit, only to find
What a mess I was in.

I tried to rise, only to learn
I was stuck to my seat.
I felt my flesh starting to burn
With insidious heat.

I kicked and I clawed at the jelly,
I fought to break out.
I gouged its eyes, elbowed its belly
And chomped on its snout.

The gelatinous thing on the chair
Laughed and swallowed me whole,
In one gulp, without pausing for air,
Took me body and soul.

Now we sit in the chair. We are one.
Won't you sit on our knee?
We care for you. It will be fun.
Just try it and see!

Kitty Hawk

Not flapping like a bird, but thrusting air
Backward at high speed from spinning blades,
The plane rolls forward, something that a pair
Of brother bicycle mechanics made.
It picks up speed. Its muslin wings slice through
The air and gently lift it up. It glides –
But no. It does not glide. It truly flies
On its own power along the beach. And so
At last man's dream of taking to the sky
Emerges in the world – is born this day.
What's more, the pilot does not crash and die
In fire like Icarus, but instead displays
Good sense, and lands. The mighty power of flight
Is given this day by Orville and Wilbur Wright.

Thanksgiving

With freedom's blessing spread upon the table,
With friends and family gathered round the feast,
We celebrate the fact that we are able
To thrive here in this boldly settled land.
Behind us lies a heritage of starving
Beneath the rule of nobleman and priest.
Before us sits a turkey we are carving
To pile meat high for every outstretched hand.

And so we thank the Pilgrims' yearning vision
That there must be a way to live anew
Where each was free to make his own decision
Of how and what to plant - and then to reap
The fruits of his own efforts - and to keep
The bounty of the harvest as his due.

Danse Macabre

The skeletons are in a dancing mood.
One grabs a violin and starts a tune
Just as the clock strives twelve. A brilliant moon
Illuminates this lively bony brood
Who leap and twirl, their spirits all renewed.
With passion that might make the living swoon,
Knowing their little jig is up too soon,
They triple-step, by icy time pursued.

A prima-ballerina leads the way,
And even as the others tire and fall,
She seems to just fly higher into space;
At last, a cock crows. Dawn. The whole mad fray
Stops dead. But then, she stands, alone of all,
And curtsies gravely, with exquisite grace.

What Child

Because we are not on this earth forever
But only for a time; because we see
Beyond ourselves to distant generations
Where others, brave and true, are yet to be;

Because we know that humankind's endeavor
Goes on and on without a stop in sight;
Because we feel that fear and desperation
Deserve to be dissolved in joyous light;

Why then we look at every newborn child
With awed respect: for each may be the one
To show the way - to shoulder weights high-piled -
To throw off burdens crushing as a ton.

Behold Man's hopes. For giant steps are all
Made by feet that once were soft and small.

Oval Beach

The lake reflects a thousand suns
As dancing, spangled waves
Concave, convex, toss back at once
The brilliance of the day.

Cavorting in the sand and spray
The children splash and catch
The liquid radiance, as their raves
Of sheer delight outstretch

The boundaries of the shore - and more
The borders of perfection,
As swooping, whooping spirits soar
In sparkling self direction.

The Leaves

The leaves fell flaming red
Like pieces of my heart.
"They're beautiful," she said,
And so we made a start

Of sifting through that treasure.
Each spangled scarlet leaf
Infused her heart with pleasure,
While I, with grateful grief,

Beheld her inner being
Still filled with bright delight.
The simple act of seeing
Outshined the looming night.

Anne

I loved to hear her talk about
      the Pennsylvania hills
Where the green trees shade the sunshine
      and the cold clear water spills
Down the slopes in twisting streamlets
      to collect in rocky pools
Where a girl could splash her cares away,
      away from all the rules
Of what to say - of what to do –
      dissolved in nature's law,
As her eyes soaked up the beauty
      and her heart filled up with awe.

In her life she bore three children,
      and taught them all she could,
And to each she passed the vision
      of that symphony in wood,
And I hear her voice to this day,
      when my wife makes ahs and oohs
As we ride across the countryside
      in search of yet more views.
That sacred spirit still lives on
      within her sons and daughter,
The spirit of that little girl,
      at play in mountain water.

Felicia

Beautiful girl, you did not get
the childhood that all your friends
experienced. No innocence
for you about the power of death
to chill the heart. Deep sorrow sends
the soul strange places. Ever since
that tragedy, you draw your breath
less evenly. It bled you, yet
you stand now, strong and competent.
Worrier - and warrior! But beneath
your poise and sharp intelligence,
my little girl is what I sense.
And my own heart is warmed to see
you growing up so gracefully,
and, dare I say, triumphantly.

Little Bird

Little bird, fly.
Take to the air.
All that life holds
Waits for you there.

Venom

Spitting venom,
Spewing vomit,
Overstuffed diamondbacks
Glisten with pain.

Listen to what the snakes sing:

> We are great critics,
> Great critics are we.
> Come lie among us
> And soon you will see
>
> That good things
> Are bad things,
>
> And bad things
> Are good.
>
> Forget what you once loved,
> And love what you should!
>
> Your natural feelings
> Will all be erased.
> Don't worry about it.
> They'll all be replaced
> With a much more acute sense of taste.

Spitting venom,
Spewing vomit,
Overstuffed diamondbacks
Writhe in the sun.

Happy are they
Who just stay away
When the snakes
Sing their songs
One by one.

Persuasion

An adjective is not an argument.
A verb does not a syllogism make.
Colorful prose may lend a rosy tint
To heaping words that mask a deep mistake.

I recognize that rhetoric is great.
It wakes up readers, makes them pay attention.
Whether you need to charm or motivate,
A metaphor or two is worth a mention.

But at the core of what you have to say,
I recommend you have some actual facts.
So when a careful jury tries to weigh
Your case they don't declare it "way too lax."

Persuasive powers alone have sometimes won,
But better to provide the smoking gun.

Medieval Memories

There's a witch of the week!
With glee they all shriek.
We'll have a fast trial
And brook no denial.
So get a rope quick
And watch the witch kick
With no chance to speak.
Die evil freak!

Assassins

The tiger cannot change her stripes
With fur of orange and black and white.

> *Furiously he sits and types*
> *A nasterpiece with lots of bite.*

The tiger roams the jungle ground
With deep green eyes that search for prey.

> *Creepily he looks around*
> *For someone new with whom to play.*

You don't have time to scream or shout.
The outcome leaves no room for doubt.
She rips you up and spits you out.

> *You're splattered with an inky blot.*
> *Your reputation's fully shot.*
> *You think he's sorry? No. He's not.*

Away

The house is cold without you.
I cranked up the A.C.
This isn't a poem about you.
It's a poem about me.

Your kitty comes around for pets
The ones she usually gets
From you. I stroke her fur
And listen to her purr.

Your maid comes in to clean.
The floors are waxed
So shiny I can almost see
My own face staring back.

You'll come home soon, and then
This place will breathe again

Whatever you do
When you come home
Don't think this poem
Is about you.

It's not. It's about me
Without you.

Thorns

I hate the thorns,
but love the rose
that so adorns
the bush - it grows
in its own way,
by its own laws -
and so I say
that just because
the petals' smell
so sweetly flows
in a drunken swell -
I love the rose
and the thorns as well.

Irish Song

I know we both think
That love should be joy.
But reach for me, girl, in your sadness.

Life's thrown us things
That should have destroyed
Any trace, any glimmer, of gladness.

But I can still sing
When you reach for your boy
And pull me back out of my madness.

The Geneticist's Love Song

I think I love your DNA
More than I love your soul.
Those twisted ladders seem to say
"Climb me, that's your goal."

I feel that all my selfish genes
Have strangely fixed on yours
As evolutionary means
By which our sort endures.

Let's research deeply, you and I,
To see if we can find
A ribosomal reason why
Our inner strands should bind.

Dear One

Dear one, dearly won,
Be near me when the day is done.
Hold me tight, and we'll ignite
A piece of midnight sun.

Reflection

Love has its secret bells,
Heard by no one else.

Deafening sounds
That shake the ground.

But only in the minds
Of those love finds.

One More

I've written many love poems – what's one more?
Some would say I've written far too many
And that it's time to stop. But it's uncanny.
Tell me "don't do it," and I go straight for
Whatever fruit's forbidden. So, stand back.
Here's one more love poem added to my pack.
Thirty years we've lived together,
Seen our share of darkest weather,
Seen our share of sunlight, too.
That's the life I've shared with you.

From the moment that we met,
I knew that I would not forget
Those sparkling eyes or ripe full lips,
Roman nose or rounded hips,
Burned into my fevered brain
There forever to remain.

When I look at you today,
I somehow see you just the way
You looked that night. It's rather strange
That I grow old and you don't change.
But if, my dear, you'd care to dance
A few more rounds, we have a chance
To see another thirty spun
One on one, around the sun.

The Wounded Wolf

The little girl who found the wounded wolf
And bandaged up its paw had made a friend
Who would not leave her. Though he seemed aloof,
He walked along beside her without end,
Quietly padding with dogged devotion,
Sniffing the air and eyeing everyone
Who came near her, and with a gentle motion
Nudging her back at times. When day is done,
He curls up next to her and feels her warmth,
And this is his idea of happiness.
His ears are tuned to listen to her heart
Pound out its beat. His tongue flicks out a kiss
Upon her cheek, and savors there the sweet
Nature that nursed him back to health again.
She falls to dreaming, safe within his den.

I Do

What can it mean to say "I do" forever?
We don't live for forever - we live now
And for some time to be, but we can never
Know with certainty the twists and turns
That lie ahead - the when and why and how
Of life's surprises - and the flame that burns
Within us for each other, hot and bright,
Might flicker and go out, or be consumed
In some new love for someone else's light.
Why would I enter into such a vow
When fortune telling is a game that's doomed?

Oh - just because of all these great unknowns
I dare to take a stand and take your hand.
We are not rolling down a hill like stones,
We do not merely bounce without a clue,
But, more like ships, we steer through storms
       toward land,
Then take to sea again - the open blue
Attracts us with its sparkling invitation
To sights unseen - to music never heard -
And not just rehash of some old sensation
But startling new experience unplanned.
Amidst all this, I offer you my word.

To keep my vessel cruising next to yours,
Whatever winds may blow, whatever gales
Wash over us - as long as mind endures -
To keep your flags in sight. For while the wind
Is what gives all the power to our sails,
It's pushing does not point our way. Unpinned
I tack against the gusting face of chance
By dint of rudders, ropes and careful craft.
I keep eyes fixed across that wide expanse
On my direction - until eyesight fails,
Though tempest tossed, though lost,
      though dazed and daft.

For like a compass pointing to the north,
The arrow in my heart points tried and true,
And by its pain I know when, back or forth,
My way has strayed from where I want to be.
All this is what I mean by my "I do."
Oh, darling, will you say the same for me?
I cannot ask for more than that you try
To keep me in your sights while yet you can.
I know that even true loves sometimes die,
But while it lives I offer mine to you:
Be my woman, and I'll be your man.

Penguin

A penguin lives in snow and ice.
He thinks the snow and ice are nice.
He jumps in cold water, just to swim.
It's very comfortable for him.
He wears a suit that's made of feathers
That keeps him warm in freezing weather.
When I get cold, I shake and turn blue,
And wish I was a penguin too.

Mild Millennial vs. Wild Perennial

In the restored Garden of Eden,
There will be no need for weedin'.
But in that perfect Zion,
I shall miss the Dandelion.

It has a witchy power.
One day it's a yellow flower.
Then, overnight, it's just
A wand of fairy dust.

Opposable

Whenever I am feeling glum,
I contemplate my opposable thumb.
It opens and closes on my command.
What a great thing to have on hand!

Explosive Puzzle

If a suicide guy went kablam in the forest
With no one to hear him - no media chorus -
No victims but trees - would he still be a terrorist?
Or would it be better to call him an errorist?

Winglift

There are so many enemies of love -
Suspicion, hurt, embarrassment, and fear
Begin the dusty list.

Yet somehow men and women rise above
Hostilities to hold each other dear,
All obstacles dismissed.

It may seem soft and dumb, like some sweet dove,
But underneath its eagle claws appear -
Difficult to resist.

Oldest Tortoise Dies

Farewell, Mr. Tortoise!
Human lives are not the shortest,
But avoiding rigor mortis
For 250 years,
Is a trick deserving cheers.